D0413265

THE DAWN OF PLANET EARTH

By Matthew Rake

Illustrated by Pete Minister

HUNGRY
TOMATO™

Everything alive today is related to life from the past.

CONTENTS

mya means 'million years ago'

Hi, My name is Ackerley and I'm an Acanthostega.

I'm your guide in this book and I have got the world's greatest story to tell you – how life evolved on Earth. Or to put it another way...

...how we all got here.

We're going to find out how tiny micro-organisms, so small you can't see them with the naked eye, evolved into huge dinosaurs. And I'll even tell you how you lot, *homo sapiens,* came into being.

But I'm getting ahead of myself.

You guys have only been around for about 200,000 years, but the world is 4,500 million years old.

If I made a 24-hour clock of the Earth's history, with the formation of the planet at midnight, the first life would appear around 4:00am, the first animals with skeletons just after 8:00pm, the first dinosaurs at 10:45pm and the first cat around 11:50pm. When would you *homo sapiens* arrive? About three seconds to midnight. That's right in the very last seconds of the very last minute of the very last hour.

So, it's a big story. In this first book, we'll see how the world was formed from nothing more than gas, dust and rocks, and how the first micro-organisms came into being.

Then I'll show you some of the first animals. This little creature is called an opabinia. And, yes, that is a claw at the end of its trunk.

How do we know this stuff?

Scientists who study the history of living things are known as palaeontologists. To learn about life in the past, they find and study fossils. Fossils are simply the remains of animals and plants that have been preserved in rocks.

There are two types of fossil: body fossils and trace fossils. A body fossil preserves the actual parts of an animal or plant. A trace fossil preserves the marks that organisms have made. For example, an animal may have made a burrow or footprints, or a plant may have left holes where its roots once were.

I'll also tell you about some of the scariest creatures, including the giant sea scorpion, a predator that grew bigger than one of you *homo sapiens,* and had claws the size of tennis rackets.

The first land animal we know of was a tiny millipede. Around 100 million years later, millipedes were growing to the size of crocodiles.

Invertebrates weren't the only animals on the land. Fish started to develop lungs and legs so they could live on land.

This is where I come in.

You see, we Acanthostegas have a big claim to fame: we were one of the first species to climb out of the water onto land.

By 250 million years ago, there existed mammal-like creatures, like Cynodont, which was a reptile that looked liked a dog (below). They became extinct in the age of dinosaurs...

...but that's another story.

Changing Shape of the Planet

You may think the map of the world has always looked the same. But the continents have changed dramatically throughout the history of Earth, just as animals and plants have. About 225 million years ago, the whole world was one big supercontinent called Pangaea.

About - 225 million years ago

About 200 million years ago, the continent of Pangaea was dividing into Laurasia in the north and Gondwanaland in the south.

About - 200 million years ago

By 65 million years ago, when the dinosaurs were wiped out, the world was looking much more like it does today. Laurasia was splitting up into North America in the west and Europe and Asia in the east. Gondwanaland had split into South America, Africa, India and Antarctica/Australia.

About - 65 million years ago

In the last 65 million years, North and South America have joined up, Antarctica and Australia separated, and India merged with the continent of Asia.

EVOLUTION TIMELINE

The story begins with the Big Bang 15,000 million years ago (mya). Life on Earth starts around 3,800 mya. Oxygen forms in the atmosphere about 2,300 mya as a waste product of photosynthesizing bacteria, in what the scientists call the Great Oxygenation Event. The ozone layer begins forming above the Earth 600 mya, this will eventually protect the Earth from the harmful rays of the sun. These events mean that animals will ultimately be able to live on the land.

The first reptiles evolve from one branch of amphibians. Reptiles are the first animals with backbones to live permanently on land. Vast forests cover the land, and these will eventually fossilize to become coal.

Sea animals start appearing in the 'Cambrian explosion of life' 540-520 mya. They swim, crawl, burrow, hunt, defend themselves and hide away. Some creatures evolve hard parts such as shells.

Life begins on land, as plants grow by lakes, streams and coasts, and arthropods (animals with segmented bodies like millipedes) venture onto land. The first jawed fish appear.

Precambrian

Cambrian

Devonian

Carboniferous

8

| Precambrian 4,540-541 mya | Cambrian 541-485 mya | Ordovician 485-443 mya | Silurian 443-419 mya | Devonian 419-359 mya | Carboniferous 359-299 mya |

The 'golden age of the dinosaurs'

witnesses huge herbivore dinosaurs feeding on lush ferns and palm-like cycads. Smaller but vicious meat-eating dinosaurs hunt the great herbivores.

Homo sapiens

appear in Africa around 200,000 years ago. By 40,000 years ago, they are also living in Europe, southern Asia and Australia. Around 16,000 years ago, they move into North America.

Dinosaurs appear,

as do the first mammals and the first flying animals with backbones, the pterosaurs.

Many different mammals evolve –

some stay on land; some, like whales, go back into the water; some, like monkeys, take to the trees.

Jurassic

Triassic

Cretaceous

Paleogene

Neogene

Quaternary

| **Permian** 299-252 mya | **Triassic** 252-201 mya | **Jurassic** 201-145 mya | **Cretaceous** 145-66 mya | **Paleogene** 66-23 mya | **Neogene** 23-2.6 mya | **Quaternary** 2.6 mya - now |

BIRTH OF THE EARTH

For millions of years, there was no life on the planet.

In fact, to begin with, there was no planet at all!

The Earth started off simply as dust and gas, spinning in a spiral. Gradually, it gathered more rocks from space, like a whirlpool funnelling more and more material into its centre.

With gravity pulling everything together, the Earth eventually became a solid planet: a great ball of molten rock and metal with a solid outer crust.

When the Earth first formed 4,540 million years ago, it was not exactly a great place for life. There was no water, no breathable air and no protection from the rays of the sun. From the inside of the planet, red-hot liquid rock, known as lava, spewed out in huge volcanic eruptions. From the outside, fiery meteorites bombarded the surface.

For life to begin, the Earth needed water. Today, water covers 70% of the planet. But where did it all come from?

Scientists once believed that as the Earth was so hot, water must have come from outside the planet. Perhaps a comet, packed with ice, crashed into the Earth. However, we can now analyse water evaporating off today's comets, and it is a different type from the Earth's.

So now many scientists think that water was trapped deep inside the planet, and forced out as steam in the volcanic eruptions. Eventually, when the Earth cooled, the steam turned to liquid water.

Precambrian 4,540-541mya

Cambrian	541-485 mya
Ordovician	485-443 mya
Silurian	443-419 mya
Devonian	419-359 mya
Carboniferous	359-299 mya
Permian	299-252 mya
Triassic	252-201 mya
Jurassic	201-145 mya
Cretaceous	145-66 mya
Paleogene	66-23 mya
Neogene	23-2.6 mya
Quaternary	2.6 mya - present

Did You Know?

As the world was full of fire and molten rock for the first 500 million years, scientists named this period the Hadean eon after the Greek god of the underworld, Hades.

The Earth's oldest known rocks are from the Hadean eon They come from Jack Hill in Western Australia and are 4,400 million years old.

11

HELL AND HIGH WATER

So how did this horribly hot and violent world change into the planet that we know, with forests, rivers and oceans bursting with all kinds of life? Well, the volcanoes created great clouds of steam; the steam collected in a thick blanket around the whole world;

and then it rained.

And when I say rain, I mean rain – a deluge that went on for thousands, perhaps even millions, of years! Think about that the next time you complain about getting caught in a passing shower.

All living things are made up of cells, the basic building blocks of life, and the first living things were composed of just one cell each. They are known as micro-organisms.

Scientists can't agree exactly where the first micro-organisms formed. Some think it was in shallow pools of seawater, some say in water droplets in the air. But the most recent theory is that life started at the bottom of the ocean, where boiling water shot up through vents from the centre of the Earth.

It doesn't sound a great place for life to exist, hundreds of metres down where no sunlight ever reaches. But the hot water bursting upwards would have carried minerals and energy to help. And anyway, the surface of the Earth was being bombarded by meteorites and covered with volcanic lava.

Today, we know that whole communities of living things – including micro-organisms, worms and giant clams - collect around the hot water of deep-sea vents.

Cambrian
541-485 mya

Ordovician
485-443 mya

Silurian
443-419 mya

Devonian
419-359 mya

Carboniferous
359-299 mya

Permian
299-252 mya

Triassic
252-201 mya

Jurassic
201-145 mya

Cretaceous
145-66 mya

Paleogene
66-23 mya

Neogene
23-2.6 mya

Quaternary
2.6 mya - present

Did You Know?

Many of the first micro-organisms, such as algae, became trapped in multiple layers of rock, known as stromatolites. In Australia, scientists have found stromatolites containing algae fossils from 3,500 million years ago. So you can actually see evidence of some of the first living things ever to appear on Earth.

A SEA CHANGE

If there were a prize for 'The Weirdest Creature That Ever Lived', **Opabinia** would be a hot favourite for the top spot. It had five mushroom-shaped eyes, 15 segments on its body, and a grasping claw at the end of a long nose (or proboscis to give it its scientific name). Opabinia used its extra proboscis to feed itself, much like an elephant uses its trunk. Perhaps it could even pull worms out of holes with its claw.

Opabinia

Another contestant for the prize of 'The Weirdest Creature That Ever Lived' would definitely be **Hallucigenia** (right). When it was first studied in the 1970s, scientists thought it walked along the bottom of the seafloor on spiny stilts, and waving tentacles grew on its back. But now experts think the tentacles were actually legs and the spines on its back provided protection. Turning it upside down might make more sense, but it still looks pretty strange!

It took about 3,000 million years for life to evolve from simple cells into soft-bodied sea animals.

That's about two-thirds of the whole age of the planet!

And what a strange-looking bunch of animals they were, when they finally did appear...

OPABINIA
Location: Canada
Length: 6cm (2.5in)

Precambrian
4,540-541mya

Cambrian
541-485 mya

Ordovician
485-443 mya

Silurian
443-419 mya

Devonian
419-359 mya

Carboniferous
359-299 mya

Permian
299-252 mya

Triassic
252-201 mya

Jurassic
201-145 mya

Cretaceous
145-66 mya

Paleogene
66-23 mya

Neogene
23-2.6 mya

Quaternary
2.6 mya - present

Hallucigenia

Did You Know?

Many of the best fossils of the earliest animals come from Burgess Shale in the Rocky Mountains in Canada. In some, you can even see the food the animal last ate inside its body – and it's over 500 million years old!

SLAYERS IN THE SEA

Soon some creatures started hunting and eating each other in the seas. They are known as predators and many of them have survived all the way through to your time.

Some, I must say, look distinctly unfriendly...

Nautiloid

Another fast and fearsome predator was the **nautiloid**. It lived inside shells and chased prey by jet propulsion. Once the nautiloid had caught up with its unfortunate victim, it would pull it into its mouth using its cluster of grasping tentacles. One species of nautiloid endoceras, grew up to 3.5 metres (11ft) long. That's the length of a Mini car!

Around 470 million years ago, the most fearsome killer was the **sea scorpion**. It could grow longer than a human and move quickly and nimbly through the water with the help of its long paddles. Then there were its deadly gripping claws: they were the size of tennis rackets and could hold prey against the sea floor before slicing and dicing!

Sea scorpion

SEA SCORPION (eurypterid)
Location: Worldwide
Length: up to 2.5 metres (8ft)

Precambrian
4,540-541mya

Cambrian
541-485 mya

Ordovician
485-443 mya

Silurian
443-419 mya

Devonian
419-359 mya

Carboniferous
359-299 mya

Permian
299-252 mya

Triassic
252-201 mya

Jurassic
201-145 mya

Cretaceous
145-66 mya

Paleogene
66-23 mya

Neogene
23-2.6 mya

Quaternary
2.6 mya - present

Did You Know?

A handful of nautiloid species exist today around Australia and the Philippines. Other sea animals that have survived from 475 million years ago include coral and sea lilies. Coral are tiny sack-like creatures that use tentacles to sweep up food.

MONSTER OF THE DEEP

The first fish emerged around 510 million years ago. They were jawless and looked like giant tadpoles. They wriggled slowly along the seabed with their mouths open, sucking up tiny animals. Over millions of years, though, they evolved jaws to bite with, forked tail fins to turn quickly, and bony heads for protection against predators, such as the sea scorpion (see previous page).

One of these bony-headed fish was the 4-tonne (8,818-lb) monster, dunkleosteus. It had an armour-plated skull about 1.3 metres (4ft) wide. The plating itself was as much as 5cm (2in) thick, and the sharpened edges of this plating served as teeth.

What's more, **dunkleosteus** had some bite, its force has been estimated at 5,000 newtons (1,100lbs). That's more powerful than the bite of today's lions, tigers or hyenas. Dunkleosteus could also open its mouth very quickly, in just one-fiftieth of a second, which created a strong suction force, pulling fast moving prey into its mouth.

WOW, look at this fellow – pretty scary, huh?

... I'm a bit worried, this monstrosity lived at the same time as me and I'd fit straight into that mouth. No wonder my ancestors adapted to escape onto land!

Dunkleosteus

DUNKLEOSTEUS
Location: Worldwide
Length: 6 metres (2oft)

Precambrian 4,540-541mya

Cambrian 541-485 mya

Ordovician 485-443 mya

Silurian 443-419 mya

Devonian 419-359 mya

Carboniferous 359-299 mya

Permian 299-252 mya

Triassic 252-201 mya

Jurassic 201-145 mya

Cretaceous 145-66 mya

Paleogene 66-23 mya

Neogene 23-2.6 mya

Quaternary 2.6 mya - present

Dunkleosteus did not have teeth. Instead it ate with the sharpened edges of bony plates around its head. These plates continued to grow as they were worn down by use. And as the top and bottom plates rubbed against each other, they were always kept sharp.

Did You Know?

Often dunkleosteus skeletons have scars that were caused by the jaws of other dunkleosteus, showing that this killer did not fear attacking its own kind!

FISH WITH FINGERS

Recognize this good-looking guy?

Yes, it's me, hanging with some of my friends down by the riverbank. We were one of the first species to develop legs. This allowed us to climb out of the water onto land.

Acanthostega

Scientists don't think acanthostega's legs could have supported its body weight, so they believe it developed them (and its fingers) to move around shallow waters filled with plants and woody debris.

So why did some fish decide that life would be better on land than in water? During the Devonian period, the Earth became warmer and drier. This meant lakes and rivers became shallower, with less oxygen and food for the animals that lived under the surface.

Some fish, known as the 'fleshy fins' or 'lobe fins', had lungs as well as gills, so they could breathe oxygen from the air. They developed muscular fins to pull themselves through shallow waters and to new pools. After many generations, these fins turned into limbs.

One of the first animals to do this was **acanthostega**. It evolved limbs and digits but not ankles and knees strong enough to support the weight of its body, so walking on land would probably have been extremely difficult!

Slightly more successful was ichthyostega, which lived at the same time as acanthostega. It hauled itself from the water using its front limbs as crutches, like a seal moves on the land today.

ACANTHOSTEGA
Length: 60cm (2ft)
Weight: about 3kg (7lbs)

Period	Time
Precambrian	4,540-541mya
Cambrian	541-485 mya
Ordovician	485-443 mya
Silurian	443-419 mya
Devonian	**419-359 mya**
Carboniferous	359-299 mya
Permian	299-252 mya
Triassic	252-201 mya
Jurassic	201-145 mya
Cretaceous	145-66 mya
Paleogene	66-23 mya
Neogene	23-2.6 mya
Quaternary	2.6 mya - present

Did You Know?

Acanthostega and ichthyostega were the first known tetrapods (animals with four feet). They are the ancestors of all the first-four-limbed animals with backbones.

THE PROMISED LAND

For over 3,000 million years, all life on Earth existed in water. Creatures could not survive on land because of the harmful ultraviolet rays of the sun. However, algae in the water produced oxygen and this eventually created a protective ozone layer around the Earth.

Then plants and arthropods (animals with jointed legs) became adapted to live on land.

Now, this story has got legs...

Millipedes thrived in the Carboniferous period as there was plenty of oxygen in the atmosphere and not many large predators. In some cases, the millipedes grew very, very large. **Arthropleura** became the size of a modern-day crocodile!

Around 440 million years ago, plants appeared on land for the first time. These were mosses and liverworts that grew flat along the ground. Cooksonia was the first plant that stood upright, with roots to take in water and tubes to carry the water to the stems.

Once plants were growing on land, they provided a food source and shelter for animals. The oldest known land animal is pneumodesmus (pronounced new-mo-des-mus), millipede that lived 428 million years ago.

ARTHROPLEURA
Location: America, Scotland
Length: Up to 2.6 metres (8.5ft)

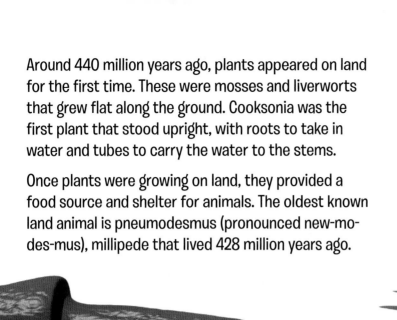

Arthropleura

Precambrian 4,540-541mya
Cambrian 541-485 mya
Ordovician 485-443 mya
Silurian 443-419 mya
Devonian 419-359 mya
Carboniferous 359-299 mya
Permian 299-252 mya
Triassic 252-201 mya
Jurassic 201-145 mya
Cretaceous 145-66 mya
Paleogene 66-23 mya
Neogene 23-2.6 mya
Quaternary 2.6 mya - present

The only known fossil of pneumodesmus was found by Mike Newman, a bus driver from Scotland. He discovered it at the seaside town of Stonehaven. 'I basically stood on it,' he said. The creature was given the full name of *Pneumodesmus newmani* in Newman's honour.

The fossil is only 1cm (0.5in) long but it is detailed enough to show spiracles: tiny holes for taking in oxygen. This proves the millipede lived on land because the spiracles would have filled up with water in rivers.

RISE OF THE REPTILES

He might look as big and ferocious as many dinosaurs, but dimetrodon was actually a reptile that evolved from early tetrapods living about 50 million years before the dinosaurs. In fact, he was more like you mammals than a dinosaur. Here he seems to have a taste for tetrapods like me.

Thank goodness he isn't around in my era

...but 70 million years later!

Reptiles were the first animals with backbones (vertebrates) able to live on land all the time. They developed scales to stop them losing water through their skin and strong legs to move around easily.

Dimetrodon

The first reptile was hylonomous. It lived 312 million years ago and was only 20cm (8in) long, including the tail. **dimetrodon** lived about 30 million years later and was about 15 times as long, making it a fearsome predator.

People have debated why dimetrodon had a 'sail' on its back. They once thought it might have been for camouflage among reeds while it waited for its prey, or to use like an actual boat sail to catch the wind while it was in the water!

Experts now think the sail might have controlled dimetrodon's body temperature. Cold-blooded reptiles need to warm up in the morning, so maybe the sail helped to soak up sunshine. Or perhaps, like the peacock's tail, it was a way of attracting mates.

Dimetrodon means 'two shapes of teeth' in Greek. At the front of its mouth were stabbing canines ideal for piercing skin. At the back, its shearing teeth sliced up bone and tough muscle. These teeth curved backwards so prey would be trapped in its mouth. The surface of all the teeth were serrated like the edge of a steak knife.

DIMETRODON
Location: America and Europe
Length: About 3 metres (11ft)

Precambrian
4,540-541mya

Cambrian
541-485 mya

Ordovician
485-443 mya

Silurian
443-419 mya

Devonian
419-359 mya

Carboniferous
359-299 mya

Permian
299-252 mya

Triassic
252-201 mya

Jurassic
201-145 mya

Cretaceous
145-66 mya

Paleogene
66-23 mya

Neogene
23-2.6 mya

Quaternary
2.6 mya - present

Did You Know?

Reptiles like dimetrodon laid their eggs on dry land, not in water like earlier tetrapods. Inside each shell, a waterproof covering, called an amnion, protected the baby and stopped it drying out.

HUNTING IN PACKS

Moschops was a reptile that did not look quite right. Its big, barrel-shaped body now seems too large for its short legs, tiny feet and little tail. However, being close to the ground meant it could graze on low-lying vegetation. And its sturdy build had another advantage: helping it withstand attacks, perhaps from a pack of cynodonts.

Moschops

Cynodont (meaning 'dog teeth') was a really mixed-up creature. Some species were carnivores, some herbivores. Some were the size of a modern domestic cat, some as large as a wolf.

Carnivorous cynodont was a fast and fierce creature. It had pointed canine teeth that could tear off chunks off flesh. Since mammals have similar teeth, scientists believe cynodonts were one of the first steps towards the evolution of mammals. Cynodont also had powerful legs under its body like a mammal, rather than at the sides like most reptiles.

Cynodont

Moschops looks as if it should be able to protect itself. It's bigger than a hippo and had a strong, hard head. In fact, I'm told moschops used their heads to butt each other and show their dominance. Well, it looks as if this particular moschops could do with

head-butting some of those cynodonts...

MOSCHOPS
Location: South African forests
Length: About 5 metres (16ft)

Precambrian 4,540-541mya

Cambrian 541-485 mya

Ordovician 485-443 mya

Silurian 443-419 mya

Devonian 419-359 mya

Carboniferous 359-299 mya

Permian 299-252 mya

Triassic 252-201 mya

Jurassic 201-145 mya

Cretaceous 145-66 mya

Paleogene 66-23 mya

Neogene 23-2.6 mya

Quaternary 2.6 mya - present

Did You Know?

During the 'Great Dying', the Permo-Triassic mass extinction, of 252 mya, 95% of all the marine species became extinct. It enabled reptiles to rule the planet.

MEET THE MAMMALS

There were all kinds of creatures around in the Triassic period. Take this chap: he might not look like it, but he's actually a reptile. And just to confuse matters further, he has a beak like a Ceratopsia dinosaur. The other little critters might look more familiar to you.

They are your ancestors

– some of the first-ever mammals to walk the Earth.

Megazostrodon

Although the Triassic period is known as the time when dinosaurs rose to dominance, it also saw the first mammals appear. They suckle their young with milk, have hair or fur, and are warm-blooded.

Scientists think little shrew-like **megazostrodon**, which appeared about 210 million years ago, may have been one of the first mammals. They believe it probably suckled its young after they hatched. Of course, scientists can't be sure, because fossils do not tell us much about how the young fed,

or whether an animal had fur or was warm-blooded.

You might think **hyperodapedon** would fancy one of those megazostrodons for lunch, especially given its fearsome beak. In fact, hyperodapedon used it to break open the seeds of now - extinct plants called seed ferns. Once the seed husk was split open, the animal chewed the softer insides at the back of its mouth so it could digest them easily.

MEGAZOSTRODON
Location: South African woods
Length: 10-12cm (4-5 in)

| Precambrian 4,540-541 mya |
| Cambrian 541-485 mya |
| Ordovician 485-443 mya |
| Silurian 443-419 mya |
| Devonian 419-359 mya |
| Carboniferous 359-299 mya |
| Permian 299-252 mya |
| **Triassic 252-201 mya** |
| Jurassic 201-145 mya |
| Cretaceous 145-66 mya |
| Paleogene 66-23 mya |
| Neogene 23-2.6 mya |
| Quaternary 2.6 mya - present |

Hyperodapedon

Not many animals fed on seed ferns, so hyperodapedon did not have to compete with other herbivores for food supplies. But, when seed ferns disappeared at the end of the Triassic period, so did hyperodapedon.

29

Hallucigenia

Pronounced: Hal-loo-si-gen-ia

For a long time, hallucigenia was thought to be an 'evolutionary misfit': not related to any other animals alive. But in 2014, scientists at Cambridge University suggested it was related to today's velvet worms, which live in tropical forests.

Sea scorpion (or eurypterid)

Pronounced: Your-rip-ter-rid

The sea scorpion's claws were equiped with long sharp spines that could have grasped even a slippery fish. They were probably designed for shooting out when close to prey, like the arms of a praying mantis.

Nautiloid

Pronounced: Nort-ill-oid

Today's nautiloids are sometimes called 'living fossils' because they have changed very little over millions of years. However, only nautiloids with curved shells, not straight ones (as on page 16) have survived.

Dunkleosteus

Pronounced: Dun-kul-oss-tee-us

Dunkleosteus was a type of fish known as a placoderm, which literally means 'plated skin'. Placoderms lasted about 50 million years. Sharks appeared at about the same time but they have survived for over 400 million years.

Arthropleura

Pronounced: Ar-thro-plur-ah

Fossil-hunters have found fossilized footprints of arthropleura, as well as fossilized body parts. They show that the giant millipede moved quickly across forest floors, swerving to avoid obstacles, such as trees and rocks.

Dimetrodon

Pronounced: Die-met-roe-don

Twenty species of dimetrodon have been found, the first one in 1878. The latest discovery is *Dimetrodon teutonis*. It was found in 2001 in Germany and is the only specimen to be found in Europe.

Moschops

Pronounced: Mo-shops

It wasn't just moschops' barrel-shaped body that made it look bizarre. Its front legs were longer than its hind legs and they sprawled outwards, like a lizard's, while the hind legs were directly under the body, like a mammal's.

Cynodont

Pronounced: Sigh-no-dont

Cynodonts had teeth like mammals: they had incisors at the front, canines at the sides and molars at the back. This is one reason why scientists think they may have beem an ancestor of mammals.

Hyperodapedon

Prounounced: High-per-oh-dap-eh-don

Hyperodapedon fossils have been found all over the area that used to be the supercontinent Pangaea. This herbivore reptile was probably a primary food source for late Triassic predators such as saurosuchus.

Megazostrodon

Pronounced: Meg-ah-zo-stroh-don

Megazostrodon evolved from cynodont. Experts believe the creature was the last step between 'mammal-like' reptiles such as cynodont, and true mammals, as like mammals, megazostrodon was warm-blooded.

INDEX

THE AUTHOR
Matthew Rake lives in London and has worked in publishing for more than 20 years. He has written on a wide variety of topics, including science, sports, and the arts.

THE ARTIST
Peter Minister started out as a special-effects sculptor and had a successful and exciting career producing sculptures and props for museums, theme parks, TV and film. He now works in CGI, which allows him to express himself with a big ball of digital clay in a more creative way than any "real" clay. His CGI dinosaurs and other animals have appeared in numerous books worldwide.